FROM THE DESERT

AMS PRESS
NEW YORK

FROM THE DESERT

BY

JOHN WESLEY HOLLOWAY

"From the desert I come to thee"—Bayard Taylor

THE NEALE PUBLISHING COMPANY

440 FOURTH AVENUE, NEW YORK

MCMXIX

Library of Congress Cataloging in Publication Data

Holloway, John Wesley.
    From the desert.

    Reprint of the ed. published by Neale Pub. Co., New
York.
    I. Title.
PS3515.0424F7   1975   811'.5'2   73-18578
ISBN 0-404-11389-3

Reprinted from the edition of 1919, New York
First AMS edition published in 1975
Manufactured in the United States of America

AMS PRESS INC.
NEW YORK, N. Y. 10003

FOREWORD

Most of my work in verse, hitherto, has been of a religious nature, samples of which may be found at the end of this volume. My preference would have been to publish that volume first, but a humor-loving public had first say. It is my firm purpose, however, to put forth, as soon as possible, a volume devoted quite, if not exclusively, to devotional, moral, and religious subjects.

THE AUTHOR

TABLE OF CONTENTS

	PAGE
INTRODUCTION	11
I AM A VOICE	13
THE MOCKING BIRD	17
THE BIRDS' QUARREL	18
THE PESSIMIST	23
MOON AND STAR	25
DISCOURAGED	27
QUILLS	29
FAERY QUEEN	31
DOWN TO FARMER JOE'S	33
PLOWIN' CANE	36
WOOD-NYMPHS	38
AUNT BETSY'S CHRISTMAS DINNER	40
SUNRISE ON THE FARM	43
THE CORN SONG	45
GARDENING	47
THE ROBIN'S LAY	49
MARRIAGE COUNSEL	52
ILL-MANNERS	54
LI'L GAL	55
CALLING THE DOCTOR	57
MAH BOY	59
JES' 'TATERS	61
MAH WIFE	62
DREAM SONG	64

PAGE

When Lindy Plays a Rag 65
The Pop-Call 67
Friendly Interest 69
Crissy 71
Youth 73
Dat Susie Gal 74
Miss Melerlee 77
Have I But You 78
The Doxology 79
The Devil 81
The Baptizing 83
The Sermon on the Mount 86
Business Religion 87
The New Preacher 89
Bap! Tism! 90
Facts About Lies 92
San Juan! 94
Black Mammies 97
Back to the Farm 100

CHILDHOOD AND YOUTH

That Fellow Behind the Glass 105
Stings 106
The Giant 107
The Poem in the Moon 108
Signposts 109
A Father's Reply to a Son's Questions 110
Drinking Song 112
On Receipt of G's Photograph 114
The Senses 115
Encourager 116

PAGE

Things Don't Stay One Way 118

Nelse 119

Whatever Is Is Best 123

Time 125

Seaward 126

Insured 127

Getting Things 128

The Iron Rule 129

The Voyage 132

A Prayer 134

Homeward 135

Baby Sister 136

War Caps 137

The Sermon and the Song 138

Sleep 139

Life 140

If We Just But Knew 141

I Rest Me in the Lord 142

Fiftieth Anniversary 143

At Twilight 144

Religious Business 146

INTRODUCTION

I AM glad to have the privilege of presenting my friend who, through the medium of these pages, will sing to you. There was a time when he had stopped singing. I am responsible for stirring him up to sing again, and therefore these pages.

He comes of a race that not only delights to sing but that sings because it must. It is said of a great singer that a man who once heard her sing remarked that her voice, while fine, was a trifle harsh. "Only let me marry her and break her heart," he said, "and she will sing with a new sweetness." The man accomplished his purpose, and it is said that after her heart had become broken the cantatrice so sang that the angels would hang over Heaven's parapets to catch the sweetness of her tones.

My friend who writes these verses has entered into the heritage of a race that is no stranger to sorrow. Thus here and there will be found the tinge of the sorrow songs of a race.

But our friend, although he has looked into the valley, has not dwelt there. Fortunately his father was a man of aspiration as well as inspiration, and always sought for his son higher light. As a result the lad had the best opportunities for education that could be obtained in schools. Yet he is not a bookworm, as these pages will show. To him commencement day was really a day for commencing his larger education. A residence in various sections of the country has given him that contact with men which is, after all, the better part of culture. There are no books like men.

Nevertheless this student and traveler is a son of the soil. After a career in the schools,—literary and professional,—after a sojourn in the cities, after a life in touch with the artificialities,—after all these things he has come back to the backwoods, to the soil, to the birds, to the animals, to the plain people Lincoln loved so well. Away down in the heart of Georgia, where one may not hear the whistle of the locomotive, I found him, with his books, his fields, his friends, his work. Here these songs were sung, and back here, away from the haunts of men, he is beating out his music.

And, as will be observed by the reader, these verses reveal the mystic. Combined with the practical wisdom of a man from the common people, and the humor of one who sees keenly the foibles and frailties of his fellow-men, will be found a vein of mysticism that sanctifies the volume. This singer sees deeper than the human eye can penetrate and enters, by means of the sixth sense, into that which is behind the veil. And in this day, when the world is torn with strife, it will be a joy to go aside and rest with this mystic in the shade of the Unseen.

In presenting John Wesley Holloway I confidently predict that his songs will receive an acceptance such as have those of no other man of his racial grouping since Dunbar's voice was stilled.

HENRY HUGH PROCTOR.

First Congregational Church,
    Atlanta, Ga.,
January 16, 1919.

I AM A VOICE

I

I AM the voice of a race of men
 Who lie at the point of death;
I hold mine ear to their fainting lips,
 To catch their dying breath.
I gather up the songs they sang
 And the words they had to say,
To hoard them till the coming time
 Brings in a better day.

I write it down,—the tale of woe
 My mother used to tell;
Record my father's story, too,
 Who stood his bondage well.
I sing the song of the cabin home
 And the banjo on the wall;
I catch the prayer of the sighing saint
 To whom "de Lawd" was all.

They one by one have laid them down
 In a low plantation grave,
Till rarely one of the host is found
 Who says: "I was a slave."

13

The red-bandana days are gone,
   Never to come again;
And the days of freedom, force, and fire
   Have dawned for this race of men.

I write for him,—the ignorant,—
   Whose true heart was not dark;
Who, though his mind was fettered fast,
   Heroic, "made his mark."
The words I write will pass away,
   His story may not die;
Sublimer bards will fashion it
   Fairer than e'er could I.

I tell of his joy when "burdened down,"
   Of his Faith when Hope was dead;
Of duty faithfully performed;
   How he bravely fought and bled;
Of his struggle to win himself a name,
   To build himself a home;
Of his sacrifice to school his child,
   Of his love for "the Kingdom Come."

"Uncle" and "Aunty," curtseying,
   No more in force appear;
But a new-born race, in a new-born world,
   In a new-born rôle, is here.
Peace to the ashes of the dead;
   Success to the brave and new;
Tears for the dying race be shed.
   Cheers for the bold and true!

II

I sing of half a hundred years,
  Now sped into the past,
To the turning-point of a world-wide war,
  That brings us peace at last;
We come at length to the Age of Gold,
  To the end of the Age of Lead;
See Phœnix Freedom rise anew,
  Out of his ashes dead!

Above a land as green, as fair,
  As ever kissed the sun,—
Nested on union, labor, thrift,
  Where the Liberty hatch was done,—
"The Eagle in a sky of blue,
  Lifts up his mighty head,
On silvery clouds of morning white,
  On gold of evening red."

Forever live, Columbia!
  Hail, hail, America!
Hail, thou who freest thyself at home,
  And champions lands afa'!
Thy stars stand in eternal blue;
  Thy bars for aye unfurled;
Thou emblem of a vision true,
  Thou hope of all this world!

America! America!
  God rest Himself in thee!
And rest thou at His Mighty Throne,
  Thou Freedom's Sovereignty!
Be armed with all thy holy might!
  Prepare Jehovah's way,
Till Justice, Peace, and Righteousness
  Hold universal sway!

THE MOCKING BIRD

HILARIOUS, bursting, bubbling thing,—
  Fountain of life and mirth,—
By night and day you sit and sing
  Carols that charm the earth!
Whence comes that bold Niagaran flood,
  Pouring in torrents down?
You gladden me, you stir my blood,
  You happy, kingly clown!

Whence? Why, you gathered all the songs
  Of all your neighbor birds,
To hymn their rights, to chant their wrongs,
  In notes too sweet for words!
The catbirds mew, the robins pipe,
  The swallows chirp anew,
And birds of every hue and type
  Find fellowship in you!

You lilt the songs of all your kind,
  Disdaining not the rote
Wherewith your comrades woo the wind,—
  Each with a single note.
A lesson learned: I'll copy you,—
  I'll gather from all men
Their softest notes, and then, I, too,
  Will pour them out again.

THE BIRDS' QUARREL

BIRDS had a quarr'l ovah hyah t'o'r night,—
  But Ah nevah quite made out de trouble—
Li'l a'ter sunset, 'bout twilight;
  My! but dey did mek a hubble!

A big man bird wid a sweet-tone voice
  Wuz a-sayin' so nice, ez 'e flew,
To putty li'l lady-bird, watchin' o' him:
  "Ah love you! Ah love you! Ah love you!"

It seem' to tek de lady-bird all b' s'prise.
  She studied hard fo' to move it,
Den h'istin' wing, flew tothah way, an' said·
  "Prove it! Prove it! Prove it!"

A middle age' lady-bird, preenin' huh wings,
  Gittin' ready to go in fo' de night,
Called to de lady-bird flyin' away:
  "You're right! You're right! You're right!"

But out f'om de pon' at de back of de lot,
  As dey bof rose higher an' higher,
A harsh rough voice screeched out f'om de mud:
  "You're a liar! You're a liar! You're a liar!"

Den a pop-eyed bird wid a topknot head,
  Lookin' almos' ez wise ez you,
Looked down in de mud at de lon'-leg t'ing,
  An' arst of 'im: *"Who? Who? Who?"*

F'om a fine young co'nfiel' ovah de way,
  Rose a bird wid a well-filled craw,
He seemed mighty anxious fo' to keep down de fuss,
  Fo' 'e kep' sayin': *"Pshaw! Pshaw! Pshaw!"*

A dainty li'l t'ing on a Cherokee rose,—
  Ve'y modes' an' gentle to me,
Wouldn' tek neithah side, but twitted 'em all,
  Sayin': *"Fiddle-de-dum! Fiddle-de-dum! Fiddle-de-dee!"*

A mothah was callin' huh wanderin' boy,
  To git 'im away f'om de fight,
So solumn dat a mockin' bird didn' mock huh,
  Ez she called out to de lad: *"Bob White! Bob White! Bob White!"*

Anothah oneasy li'l ma'am cried out,—
  'Bout huh husban', 'twas easy to see,—
To a scared li'l Bobby Bird whirrin' away:
  "Wait — fo' Mr. McCree! Wait — fo' Mr. McCree!"

Dat minute Ah notussed a sparkin' young pa'r,
   In de top of a deep leafy dome;
Didn' see whut de fellar had done, but she wailed:
   "You're a naughty boy! Ah'm gwine home!"

An' ol' mo'h'r Ree wuz callin' huh Jo,—
   Not anxious,—Ah'm boun' to agree;
Ah jedge she wuz ig'nant o' trouble gwine on,
   Fo' she quietly called: *"Jo Ree! Jo Ree!"*

An' all dis time a ciccady ban'
   Wuz a-chunnin' up in de trees;
An' a *do-re-mi* concert out by de pon'
   Wuz a-movin' along wid ease.

But de fuss kep' a-growin', gittin' higher an' higher,
   Till a bird sung out in a treble,
Lightin' in a cedar tree ovah mah head:
   "Kick lak de debul! Kick lak de debul!"

Again f'om de wise one: *"Who? Who? Who?"*
   Fo' answer echoed de treble,
'Way cross de rice pon' ovah de swamp:
   "Kick lak de debul! Kick lak de debul!"

A batch'ler maid in a willer tree,
   Whar 'is ugly words could reach 'er,
Woke up wid a start an' a pious scream,
   Ez she hurried out: *"Preachah! Preachah!
   Preachah!"*

A weak voice asked: *"W'at's 'at? W'at's 'at?"*
  Seemin'ly wantin' to he'p 'ah;
Till a strong one answerin', knowin'ly said:
  "She's peppah! She's peppah! Peppah!"

De sparrer was boostin': *"Peace! Peace! Peace!"*
  De ducks an' geese come flockin';
But de cry was drowned by a big flock o' geese,
  An' de peckah-wood was knockin'.

De owl *ha! ha'd!* de catbird hissed!
  A rain-crow Ah recall;
A bull-bat, too, was dippin' in,
  An' de blue jay, meanes' of all.

But Ah wuz 'temptin' to 'termine de side,
  Whar de kick-bird wuz tekin' 'is stan';
An' 'e didn' tell me, an' 'e didn' tell de owl,
  Wid de scrap spreadin' ovah de lan'.

But Ah made up mah min',—don' know 'bout de
      owl,—
  Dat w'enevah yo' git into trouble
Smooth it all off jest ez nice ez yo' can,
  If yo' mus' kick, kick lak de debul!

Oh, dis worl's a fussy an' a funny ol' worl',
  Whut time yo' don' hafter grieve 'ere,
Fo' jes' den de clock on de mantel struck twelve,
  Ez Ah heard: *"Yo' gotta l e a v e 'ere! Yo' gotta
      l e a v e 'ere!"*

Den Ah t'ought on life, an' Ah t'ought on deat',
  T'ings dat always puzzles mah head;
But Ah quieted down wid de frogs an' de birds,
  An' Ah ambled off to bed.

THE PESSIMIST

Hit's a crime to steal a chicken,
    So de starvin' poo' are taught;
'Tain't no crime to steal a million,—
    All de crime's in gittin' caught.

'Sright to undermine yo' neighbor,
    Spile his business if yo' can;
Tumble down his reputation,
    Only,—do it lak a man.

Seems to be a sacred duty
    Fo' de rich to 'press de poo';
But it's wrong to kick yo' neighbor,
    Till he's prone upon de floo'.

Poo' man got to go it 'umble,
    Till 'e git de upper han',
Den 'e got to sco'n de people,
    W'at don't own no house an' lan'.

'Tain't no harm to shoot a robin
    Singin' merry on de tree;
Hit jes' spo't to kill a rabbit,
    Hit jes' fun to rob a bee.

Blue grass 'posin' on de meadah,
   Cattle 'posin' on de grass;
Poo' man 'posin' on de cattle,
   An' de rich man on de mass.

Well, Ah'm feelin' kind o' t'irsty;
   Here's a watermelon patch!
Guess Ah'll 'pose upon somebody,—
   'Thout Ah meet up wid mah match.

MOON AND STAR

(The night of May 5, 1916)

O MOON and Star,
How fair you are,
Up there in the sky!
Sky so blue,
Golden, too,
Underneath the two of you.

Twilight fades;
Deeper shades
Gather in the trees;
Moon and star
Brighter are
In the sky afar.

How you glow,
Bright as snow
In a streak of light!
Pale the rest,—
E'en the best,—
All eyes seek the west!

First o' May,
Lovely day,
Night calm and serene;

Blooming trees,
Swarming bees,
Green lawns, grassy leas!

Yard apart,
Head and heart,
Just you two up there;
Shine together,
Crown the weather,
Springtime everywhere!

DISCOURAGED

Tell yo' what, mon, Ah'm discouraged!
  Been a man since forty-fo';
Nevah had de luck Ah'm havin',
  Since Aun' Katy barred de doo'.
Rain a-fallin' ever' mornin',
  Storm a-comin' ever' night;
Nevah see sich nasty weathah,
  Since de Lawd gi' me mah sight!

Boll-worm eatin' up de cotton;
  Mildew eatin' up de co'n;
'Taters in de groun' a-rottin',—
  Wush ol' Gabul blow 'is ho'n!
Colry killin' off de cattle;
  Rabbits eatin' up mah peas;
Some on' stealin' all mah mellins;
  Chickens dyin' wid disease.

Can' stir roun' fo' so much watah,—
  Settin' roun' bof night an' mo'n,—
Grass a-growin' lak de dickuns,
  Woe is me dat Ah wuz bo'n!
Dar's dat sto' man actin' funny,
  Othah's pressin' fo' deir pay;
If Ah had a little money,
  Fo' de Lawd, Ah'd run away!

Cross ol' 'oman, bawlin' chil'en,
    To mah finish sholy p'ints;
'Sides, Ah feel mos' lak Ah'm dyin',
    Wid dis mis'ry in mah j'ints;
'Clar' to goodness Ah'm discouraged!
    Dough Ah'm Christ'an thu an' thu,
Le' me have a jug o' licker,
    Ain' no tellin' what Ah'd do!

QUILLS

Oh, de banjer's fo' de cabin,
　　An' de bones is fo' de pan,
De guitar's fo' de pahlah,
　　An' de drum is fo' de ban';
But dar is a kind o' music dat des suits de woods
　　　　an' hills:
　　Hit's a *whoop!* an' a *toot!*
　　An' a picanin' to boot,
Wid a *"Oo-lalla-oo!"* to de quivah of de quills!

W'en yo' hyah it in de mornin',
　　Erbout de break o' day,
'Way ovah cross de meadahs,
　　A mile or two away,
Yo' c'n hol' yo' bref an' lis'n till yo' livah fairly
　　　　th'ills!
　　Hit's a *whoop!* an' a *toot!*
　　An' a nappy head to boot,
Wid a *"Oo-lalla-oo!"* to de quivah of de quills!

Yo' c'n break up de pianny!
　　T'row de organ in a heap!
De banjer, bones, an' guitar's
　　Plenty good ernough to keep!

But de whistle of de fores' an' de chatter of de
         rills
    Is a *whoop!* an' a *toot!*
    An' a raggedy rat to boot,
Wid a *"Oo-lalla-oo!"* to de quivah of de quills!

To me hit's jest a mem'ry
    Of w'en Ah wuz a boy:
Ah used to hyah it ever' day,
    An' ever' time wid joy!
Hit 'uz better dan a doctor wid a coffin-full o'
         pills:
    'Twas a *whoop!* an' a *toot!*
    An' a woolly head to boot,
Wid a *"Oo-lalla-oo!"* to de quivah of de quills!

FAËRY QUEEN

MERRILY and cheerily
  O'er the hill she comes;
Prettily and wittily
  Through the grove she hums.

Hurriedly and flurriedly
  O'er everything she runs,
Making billows on the wheat,
  And turning eyes to suns.

Easily and pleasingly
  She bids us be polite,
Or else she'll take our hats away
  And keep them off till night.

Blund'ringly and wond'ringly
  We ask her whence she comes;
Smilingly, beguilingly,
  She shakes her head and hums.

Playfully and gayfully
  She courts a pretty cloud;
And when he makes an awkward move,
  She always laughs aloud.

Willfully and skillfully
  The sparrow leaves her nest,
And flying to the Faëry's,
  It twitters on her breast.

Knowingly and showingly
  Calm Nature likes her touch,
For every time she passes by,
  His looks improve so much!

Faëry Queen, Faëry Queen,
  We bless you every day!
We long to feel your tender touch
  When you are far away!

But you will come again in spring,
  With all your old sweet way;
For, dear, you are no other than—
  Miss Pleasant Breeze of May!

DOWN TO FARMER JOE'S

It's a happy time an' hearty,—
  Ever'body goes,—
When dar's gwine to be a pahty
  Down to Fahmah Joe's.

He jes' chins up to his fiddle,
  An' 'e gits 'is heel a-gwine,
Pulls de bow across de middle,
  An' 'e sets dat t'ing a-cryin'!
W'en yo' ketch yo'se'f you're amblin'
  To de middle o' de floo',
Wid yo' pardner round a-ramblin'
  To de call o' Fahmah Joe.

Hear 'im holler, "Swing de co'nahs!"
  "Ladies, sachez back again!"
"Gent'men, give yo' ladies honahs!"
  "Ever'body balancin'!"
W'en yo're standing still, yo're jumpin'
  In de middle o' de air,
Clappin' han's,—an' how yo're humpin'!
  Feel jes' lak yo' got to r'ar!

Got to smile roun' at yo' lady;
    Got to take huh by de arm;
Got to cake walk whar it's shady,
    Down to Uncle Joie's fahm.
B'mbye de rooster crows fo' midnight,
    Den Aun' Judy teks a han';
"Come," she says, "an' gi⁺ a li'l bite!"—
    Not'in finer in de lan'!

W'en it's ovah, back to dancin';
    "One mo' set befo' yo' go!"
Sich anothah jinks an' prancin'
    Roun' dat ol' log-cabin floo'!
All de gals git lookin' at yo',
    Smilin' sweet an' lovin', too;
Boys a-frownin', sayin', "Drat yo'!"
    An' dey're hintin' roun' at you.

Den you holler out, "Ah'm goin'!"
    Flingin' open wide de doo';
All de gals come round you flowin',
    In a grea' big ring,—jes' so!
Lak a prince you walk among 'em,
    As dey scuffle fo' yo' ahm;
Tho de othah fellars brung 'em,
    You're deir doughty champion.

Off you march in all yo' glory,
    Lookin', feelin', brave an' bol',
Tho you feel anothah story
    Mus' be swiftly, quickly told.

Soon de naughty fellows shock yo'
    W'en dey yell wid dreadful soun';
Den dey stay behin' an' rock yo',
    Ever' blessed step to town.

You jes' herd yo' flock an' leave 'em,
    Each one at huh mothah's doo';
An' yo' do yo' bes' to grieve 'em,—
    T'ings yo' got to undergo.
But it's not de boys dat git yo'
    W'en yo' thoo yo' winder creep,—
It's yo' mammy's rattan hit yo',
    W'en yo' t'ought huh fast asleep.

But yo' hardly feel de whiskin',
    An' yo' sca'cely min' de blows;
Fo' yo' heart is dancin', friskin',
    Wid de gals at Fahmah Joe's.

PLOWIN' CANE

Hol' up yo' haid, ol' mule, I say!
I know you t'ink dis cane is hay,
You're trained to leave dat co'n alone,
But dis 'ere cane's anothah one:
'Twan't made fo' mules, hit's made fo' men;
An' don't you bite dat stuff again!
Hit's strange to me dat you don' know
Hit's bettah to let de green t'ings grow
Till harves' time; hit's sweeter den,
Besides, 'twill be as much again.
But you'd bite down de growin' grain,
An' starve w'en snowflakes sweep de plain.
But I don' know. Perhaps to God
I'm bad as you. Hit's mighty odd,
But lots o' t'ings I should leave alone
Till harves' time, I bite 'em down;
And fruits He meant fo' 'ternity,
I t'ink are none too good fo' me.
I go to war an' shoot His men;
I kill His oaks an' feel no sin:
If I was wise an' jes' but knew,
Dar's worse'n dat I 'spec' I do,—
Lay rash han's on His treasures rare,
An' de angels wonder how I dare.
An' I been taught temptation's way,

36

To watch an' fight, an' strive, an' pray;
But you ain' had no teachin' 'tall,
An' I'm yo' God,—but dat ain't all:
You know yo' right to a wisp o' hay,
An' yo' t'ink you're robbed o' your lawful prey
W'en I mek yo' leave dis sorghum be,
An' I know you t'ink it's mean o' me.
Well, eat some mo'; we'll soon be done;
A mule deserves a little fun;
An' may my God look on me, too,
Jes' lak I'm lookin' on to you!

WOOD-NYMPHS

Oh, I know a shady nook,
  Where the saucy wood-nymphs play;
Through it runs a babbling brook,
  Whither gentle breezes stray.
Violets deck its mossy sides,
  Sparrows twitter in the trees;
Sweet it murmurs as it glides
  Gently o'er the mossy leas.

It is there that life is sweetest,
  When the flowers are bathed in dew;
Nature's joys are then completest,
  When the day is bright and new.
Oh, the wood-nymphs are beguiling,
  And they charm my senses so!
For, anon, I catch me smiling
  O'er some scene of long ago.

All the sweetest days of childhood,
  All the things I loved most dear,
Rise before me in this wildwood,
  Bringing light and hope and cheer:
Schooldays, parties, notes, and glances,
  Moonlight rides through wood and glade,
Fiddler Bob's and merry dances,
  Happy strolls in sun and shade!

Dear old faces rise before me,
   In the gladness of this hour;
All the charm of youth steals o'er me,
   With its strange, unearthly power.
There was Hester! How I loved her!
   She, my first and purest joy!
But, alas! aside I shoved her
   When she loved another boy!

There were Sallie, Susie, Carrie,
   With each once I played the dunce;
But I none of them would marry,—
   Man can never love but once.
Hark! The sun is mounting higher;
   I must leave this bosky dell!
Schooltime draws each moment nigher—
   Horrors! There's the breakfast bell!

AUNT BETSY'S CHRISTMAS DINNER

Guess Ah'll set hyah at de en',—
　　Plenty elbow room!—
Been gwine hongry two, t'ree days,
　　Waitin' fo' dis to come!
An' since de blessin' done been ax',
　　An' business set a-gwine,
Let ever'body he'p hisse'f,
　　Ah'm gwine on down de line!

Aun' Betsy's Chris'mas dinners, mon,
　　Yo' nevah see de beat!
Whoevah gits a chance to come,
　　Gits w'at 'e wants to eat!
She sholy hit me right dis time,
　　De way mah honger leans;
Jes' he'p mah plate up good an' strong
　　To dat bacon an' dem greens!

De way she beats a biscuit, sah,
　　An' bakes a pone o' bread,
An' brews a bar'l o' simmon beer.
　　'Ould tu'n a prince's head!
My goodness!—uh, uh!—Hyah dey come,
　　Hot Yankee po'k an' beans!
Ah know Aun' Betsy cooks 'em good,
　　But—*Pass me back dem greens!*

A Frenchman couldn' brown a fish
　　De way Aun' Betsy can;
An' de way crab gumbo acts fo' huh—
　　W'y, honey, it beats de ban'!
Dat chicken roas' 'ould mek a dish
　　'At's fit fo' kings an' queens;
Aun' Betsy's han's is prime at dat,
　　But—*Shove me back dem greens!*

Dat coffee smoke 'ould mek yo' smile,
　　As fur as you c'n smell;
But w'n yo' scent huh chicken pie,
　　Hit hot an' pipin',—well!
An' sassage sniffin' thyme an' sage,
　　Han'-stuffin',—no machines,
An' hot fried chicken, Glory be!
　　But—*Jes' once mo', dem greens!*

An' w'en she boils a pot o' rice
　　An' puts de gravy in,
De man dat tu'ns his back on dat,
　　He mos' commits a sin!
Dat possum wid dem 'taters roun'
　　Jes' fits mah cut o' jeans;
Not quite ready fo' 'im yet,
　　Jes'—reach me roun' dem greens!

An' w'en she smoke an' fry a ham,
　　Or bile 'im till 'e cream,
Jes' shet yo' eyes an' go to sleep!
　　Hit sholy is a dream!

Dem chitlin's, long wid cracklin' bread,
 Remin' me o' mah 'teens;
La! la! dey's good,—Ah know dey is!
 But—*Please, ma'am, pass dem greens!*

Ah wush Ah wuz a elerphunt,
 Ah'd do dis dinner jus'!
Ain' got no room fo' not'n' else,—
 Ah gotta quit or bus'!
One little tas'e o' 'tater pie—
 Ah'll resk dem colic peens—
But won't you pass dat pan once mo'?
 Ah'll finish up dem greens!

SUNRISE ON THE FARM

Sich a singin' in de trees!
Sich a hummin' o' de bees!
Sich a sweet an' holy calm!
Roun' de meadows cowbells ring,
Stirrin's ever' livin' thing,
W'en yo' wake at daybreak,—fo' sunrise on
de farm.

Kittens purrin' at yo' leg,
Puppies prancin'—on de beg,
Pidgins lightin' on yo' arm,
Daisies bloomin' at yo' feet,
Dewy grass and roses sweet,
W'en yo' come downstairs at daybreak on
de farm.

Pigs a-squealin' in de pen,
Heifers lowin' to git in,
Biddies scootin' 'way f'om harm;
Dobbin swishin' at de flies,
Bats a-flappin' 'cross de skies,
W'en yo' walk abroad at sunrise on de farm.

Far away de river flowin',
Here an' yonder rooster crowin',—
Noises full o' soothin' balm;—
    Sich a click an' clack an' clutter!
    Sich a flip an' flap an' flutter!
W'en yo' 'proach de barnyard at feed-time
        on de farm.

Catbird callin' to his mate,
June-bug buzzin' th'u de gate—
W'at enchantment! W'at a charm!
    Mocker trillin' in de glen!
    Blue-jay, swallow, coot, an' wren
Greet yo' happy ears at sunrise on de farm.

Feed de chickens, milk de cows,
    Hitch de mules up to dem plows,—
Sun's a-shinin' bright an' warm!
    Eat a bite, an' kiss de pump,—
    Bet yo' life yo' got to hump,
W'en it's plantin' time at sunrise on de farm!

THE CORN SONG

Jes' beyan a clump o' pines,—
  Lis'n to 'im now!—
Hyah de jolly black boy,
  Singin', at his plow!
In de early mornin',
  Thoo de hazy air,
Loud an' clear, sweet an' strong,
  Comes de music rare:

    "O mah dovee, Who-ah!
      Do you love me? Who-ah!
        Who-ah!"
    An' as 'e tu'ns de cotton row,
      Hyah 'im tell 'is ol' mule so;
      "Whoa! Har! Come 'ere!"

Don't yo' love a co'n song?
  How it stirs yo' blood!
Ever'body list'nin',
  In de neighborhood!
Standin' in yo' front doo'
  In de misty mo'n,
Hyah de jolly black boy,
  Singin in de co'n:

"O Miss Julie, Who-ah!
Love me truly, Who-ah!
Who-ah!"
Hyah 'im scol' 'is mule so,
W'en 'e try to mek 'im go:
"Gee! Whoa! Come 'ere!"

O you jolly black boy,
Yod'lin' in de co'n,
Callin' to yo' dawlin',
In de dewy mo'n,
Love 'er, boy, forevah,
Yodel ever' day;
Only le' me lis'n,
As yo' sing away:

"O mah dawlin'! Who-ah!
Hyah me callin'! Who-ah!
Who-ah!"
Tu'n aroun' anothah row,
Holler to yo' mule so:
"Whoa! Har! Come 'ere!"

GARDENING

Oh, what joy in merry Maytime,
  In the merry morning, too,
Just to walk abroad at gray time,
  When the grass is laved in dew!—
Just to walk among your flowers,
  Hovered o'er with buzzing wings,
There to spend the cheerful hours,
  Lookin' at the growin' things!

How the collards are a-jumpin'!
  How the pea-vines spread around!
How the lettuce is a humpin'!
  How the squashes kiver groun'!
Goodness, how the grass is growin'!
  Wow!—that nettle—how it stings!
Bugger! You shan't git a showin'
  With my precious growin' things!

There's a lily bowin' at you,
  With a gauze-wing poising near;
Blooming zinnias! There's a,—drat you!—
  Black gnat thund'rin' in my ear!
Just a little wind and weather,—
  Just the kind that kind o' clings,—
Till the rain has soaked the heather,
  Then you'll see some growin' things:

English pease and greens for dinner,
    Cauliflower and new potatoes.
Make these beets a little thinner,
    Gather in these red tomatoes.
What is life without a garden,
    And the good things Maytime brings,
As you watch the soft stems harden
    And you grow with growin' things?

THE ROBIN'S LAY

Oh, I breathe the balmy air,—
  As I sing, as I sing,—
Skimming through the sky so fair,
  As I sing.
Sweet I sniff the gentle breeze,
As it wafts among the trees,
To the hum of busy bees,
  As I sing.

I am working with a will,—
  As I sing, as I sing,—
In a willow by the mill,
  As I sing.
I am doing there my best,
As I build my cosy nest,
Though I never stop to rest
  As I sing.

How I make the echoes ring,—
  As I sing, as I sing,—
Nature seems a living thing,—
  As I sing.
When I fly across the dell,
And I see that all is well,
Joys I feel that none can tell,
  As I sing.

49

I am happy all the day,—
   As I sing, as I sing,—
Swiftly flee the hours away,
     As I sing.
I see such delicious things,
Where the ripples part in rings,
While I preen my pretty wings,
     As I sing.

Ah! and now my nest is done!—
   As I sing, as I sing,—
And the eggs in it are one,
     As I sing.
I am happy more and more,
For the one has changed to four;
I shall have some birdies, sure,
     As I sing.

I am staying now at home,—
   As I sing, as I sing,—
Mother birds should never roam,
     Though they sing.
Now I see my grand array,
As they all around me play;
Oh, what sweetness they display,
     As I sing.

Soon they'll flit from tree to tree,—
   As I sing, as I sing,—
Soon they'll wander far from me,
     As I sing.

Soon they'll build their own sweet
        home,
    Resting near its palace dome,
    When the springtime days are come,
        As I sing.

Ah, the frost has come again,—
    As I sing, as I sing,—
And the forest trees complain,
        As I sing.
He has stripped those pretty trees,
He has shaken off their leaves.
How it all my spirit grieves,
        As I sing!

Life is coming to an end,—
    As I sing, as I sing,—
Death is flying in the wind,
        As I sing.
Well I know that winter's near.
I must take my leave of here,
Far away my course to steer,
        As I sing.

MARRIAGE COUNSEL

De bride an' groom will stan' apart,
An' put yo' right han' on yo' heart;
De answer dat Ah ax of you,
In ever' case mus' all be true.

Will yo' tek dis gal fo' to be yo' bride,
An' keep huh close up by yo' side,
Don't be 'lowin' huh to gad erbout,
Wid huh haid tied up, an' huh heels tu'ned
    out,—
To be telling' huh lies f'om doo' to doo',
An' lis'enin' out fo' to hyah 'em grow?
Ef yo' c'n give an answer true,
Jes' speak right out an' say: "Ah do!"
Will yo' dress huh poo' an' feed huh slim,
Ef chil'en come, mek huh feed dem?
Drink up yo' wages, stay out at night,
An' ef she cheeps, start up a fight?
Ef yo' c'n give an answer still,
Jes' speak up loud an' say: "Ah will!"

Will yo' tek dis man fo' to be yo' groom,
An' follow 'im cl'ar up to de tomb,
Collec' his policies den an' dar,
An' set right out fo' to be a b'ar?

Wear black to show yo' is beref',
But spen' yo' greenbacks right an' lef',
Stay on de kyars f'om night till mo'n,
An' don't stop gwine till all is gone?
Ef yo' c'n give an answer true,
Jes' speak right out an' say: "Ah do!"

An' while he's livin' will yo' keep 'im hot,
Whedder he's good or bad or not,—
Vex 'im ontill 'e knocks yo' down,
Den air de matter in co't, in town?
Won't cook his vittles nor patch 'is pants,
An' save yo' smiles fo' de young gallants?
Ah ax dese t'ings,—Ah put yo' wise:
Ah don' want to hyah yo' tell no lies.
Ef yo' c'n give an answer still,
Jes' speak up loud an' say: "Ah will!"

Now jine yo' han's an' hol' 'em fas',
Or de debil'll git yo' bof at las'.

Now Ah condemn yo' man an' wife,
Bof o' yo' to serve fo' life!
Jes' pass me ovah six bits toll,
An' de Lawd have mussy on yo' soul!

ILL-MANNERS

LAND o' goodness! Sakes o' livin'!
  W'at yo' startin' now?
Look here, mister, whar's yo' raisin'?
  Whar yo' f'om, nohow?

Haid look lak a bar'l o' wisdom,
  Dressed up lak a prince;
Speak jes' lak a walkin' grammah,
  Still ain' got no sinse!

Stranger, too, Ah wouldn' know yo',
  One man from anothah;
W'at you said Ah wouldn' tek, sah,
  F'om mah own deah brothah!

Been to school, Ah bet a dollar;
  Got a sheepskin soakin';
Still ain't learnt dar's lots o' t'ings
  Dat won't stan' no jokin'!

W'en a man wants fowl an' rice,
  Jest 'e signerfy!
Not be arstin' pu's'nal questions,—
  I da sell, he buy!

Man yo' age an' green as you is,
  Ought to have a lickin'!
Don' know no better'n ax a man
  Whar he gits a chicken!

LI'L GAL

COME to yo' daddy, Li'l Gal,
O you baddy, li'l gal.
W'at yo' been doin' since dad been gone,
To gethah his baby gal some co'n?
Rompin' in de san' an' playin' in de hay;
Hyah dat w'at yo' mammy say?
O you li'l mischief,
   Sugar Ba'!

O you darlin' Li'l Gal,
Stop dat quarr'lin', li'l gal;
Fussin' fo' candy,—oh dat's rough!
Seems to me you're sweet ernough!
Now gi' me a bite an' le' me see
Jes' how sweet li'l gals can be!
Tas'e lak 'lasses,
   Honey Bee!

One mo' buss, mah Li'l Gal,
See yo' done muss me, Li'l Gal,—
'Lasses streak f'om mouth to eye,
Ah'm gwi' eat you, Sugar Pie!
When yo' done eat yo' milk an' bread,
Better git ready an' go to bed,
Or boogar man git you,
   Sleepy-head!

"Now I lay me," Li'l Gal,
Le' me hyah yo' say me, Li'l Gal,
Shet yo' eye, an' fol' yo' han',
Speak out loud an' say, "Aman!"
Now kiss dad an' mam good-night,
Clamb in yo' cradle an' quirl up tight,
God A'mighty bless yo',
    Li'l Mite!

CALLING THE DOCTOR

Ah'm sick, doctor-man, Ah'm sick!
Gi' me some'n' to he'p me quick,
   Don't,—Ah'll die!

Tried mighty hard fo' to cure mahse'f;
Tried all dem t'ings on de pantry she'f;
Couldn' fin' not'in' a-tall would do,
   An' so Ah sent fo' you.

"Wha'd Ah take?" Well, le' me see:
Firs',—horhound drops an' catnip tea;
Den rock candy soaked in rum,
An' a good sized chunk o' camphor gum;
Next Ah tried was castor oil,
An' snakeroot tea brought to a boil;
Sassafras tea fo' to clean mah blood;
But none o' dem t'ings didn' do no good.
Den when home remedies seem to shirk,
Dem pantry bottles was put to work:

Blue-mass, laud'num, liver pills,
"Sixty-six, fo' fever an' chills,"
Ready Relief, an' A. B. C.,
An' half a bottle of X. Y. Z.

An' sev'al mo' Ah don't recall,
Dey nevah done no good at all.
Mah appetite begun to fail;
Ah fo'ced some clabber, about a pail,
Fo' mah ol' gran'ma always said
When yo' can't eat you're almost dead.

So Ah got scared an' sent for you.—
Now, doctor, see what you c'n do.
Ah'm sick, doctor-man, Gawd knows Ah'm sick!
Gi' me some'n' to he'p me quick,
    Don't,—Ah'll die!

MAH BOY

Lady, don' was'e yo' bref
    Complainin' o' dat li'l boy;
Ah know 'im better'n you evah could:
He's de baddes' boy in de neighborhood;
He ain' good-lookin', an' 'e ain' no good;
    Sometimes 'e pesters me mos' to def,
    Hardly an ounce o' patience lef',—
        Yet he's mah earthly joy!

I know he's "black and rough,"
    An' "dirty as he can be";
He's de sneakinis' kind of a little liar,
His soul ain' fit fo' not'n' but fiah,
Dar's not'n' in him dat you'd admire,
    Ah know he's worritted you ernough,
He's lak you say, "a little tough,"—
        But world an' all to me!

Some'n' you-all don' know:
    He ain' nevah had no pa:
He died an' lef' 'im six weeks ol';
Lef' us bof out in de col';
But de saddes' part Ah nevah tol',—
    De li'l ol' t'ing, Ah loved 'im so!—
    Ah nevah mentioned it befo',
        He saved his tempted ma!

Mebbe he'll change some day, —
'Twould be mah greatest joy;
Ah'm prayin' to God to bring it about;
Ah know it's comin', widout a doubt;
An' when it comes Ah'll raise a shout;
But if 'e got hung Ah'd love 'im a'way,
An' Ah don' keer what othahs say,—
Fo' he's mah boy!

JES' 'TATERS

Aн know all erbout good eatin',
An' 'tain't wuth while repeatin',
Bac'n and greens, an' pot-roas' brisket,
Ham an' eggs an' beaten biscuit,
Chitlins an' co'n bread, chicken an' rice,
All dem t'ings is mighty nice;
'Possum an' taters'll do to eat,
But Ah don' know not'n' 'tall to beat
   Jes' 'Taters!

Let 'em stay in de groun' till de black-fros'
     come,
Den yo' dig 'em up an' yo' haul 'em home;
Yo' bank 'em till dey git all good an' sweet,
An' den yo' got some'n' 'at's good to eat;
W'en yo' bake 'em in de oven, dey juice de
     pan;
Roas' 'em in de ashes dey beat de ban';
Butter 'em hot, or eat 'em col',
Dey reach a spot down in yo' soul;
Eat 'em f'om de table, or tek 'em f'om de hob,
Midnight or noon, hit's a mighty fine job.
Yo' c'n tek all othah t'ings away,
An' gi' me a feas' t'ree times a day,—
   Jes' 'Taters!

MAH WIFE

Mah wife's de meanes' 'oman evah
    Come along since Eve!
Set huh up agin' de worl',
    She'd win, Ah do believe!
She meks a lovely livin', an'—
    She lets me draw de pay;
But she keeps huh red rag runnin'
    In a dev'lish sort o' way!

It's allus: "Money, money, money!"
    F'om dark to settin' sun!
An' Ah can' bear up no longah, dough—
    Ah nevah give 'uh none.
Ah've seen a lot o' womenkin',
    But Ah nevah see' huh match!
Fussin' comes as nat'al to huh
    As it do fo' a hen to scratch!

Ah'm gwine erbout divorcin' 'uh!
    Ah'll have 'uh 'fore de law!
She'll cook an' wash an' iron good,
    But,—golly! how she jaw!
She's a bear-cat wid dat tongue o' hern,
    By any kind o' make!
An' since she's hoss too ol' to ben',
    She's colt ernough to break!

Ah jes' can' stan' 'uh! No, sah,—Ah
      won't!—
  Dat 'oman gotta go!
If huh home is in Missouri,
  Ah'm jes' right here to show—
W'at dat yo' say? "What kind o' fool?"
   Mah wife? Of all de brass!
Don' t'ink Ah'm one to stan' an' tek
  Yo' impudence an' sass!

How dare you say sich ugly t'ings?
  Erbout mah lovin' wife?
      Tek dat,—an' dat!
      Pick up yo' hat!
Nex' time Ah ketch yo' 'busin' huh,
  Ah'll whet mah kyarvin' knife!

DREAM SONG

Teardrops fill mine eyes, sweetheart,
  Whene'er I think of you,
Your loving lips, your sparkling eyes,
  Your tender heart and true!
Your gentle voice still thrills my soul,
  As in the days gone by;
As when we wandered side by side
  Together, you and I.

I see you dressed in white, sweetheart,
  A rosebud in your hair
That glistens like an aureole
  Above your brow so fair.
You hold your bonnet by a string;
  A smile lights up your eye;
As side by side in merry May,
  We wandered, you and I.

Long years have come and gone, sweetheart,
  But still I mourn for you;
The world of men has all proved false,
  And you alone are true;
Mine eyes are dimming to the world,
  But sparkling to the sky,
And soon we'll wander once again
  Together,—you and I.

WHEN LINDY PLAYS A RAG

Chacun à son goût.

I HAVE listened to de masters,
   I have hyard de Navy Ban';
I have hyard de fines' singers,
   Evah traveled thoo de lan';
I have seen de bonny Scotsman
   Playin' pibrochs on his bag;
But I ruther set an' lis'n
   When Lindy plays—a rag!

I have hyard de banjo ringin',
   "Jes' beside de cabin doo'";
I have hyard de darkies wingin'
   Roun' de ol' log cabin floo';
I have hyard de big pipe organ
   Mek de rafters crack an' sag;
But yo' nevah hyard no music
   Till Lindy plays—a rag!

Fust, yo' feels yo' pulses quicken,
   Den yo' break into a smile;
Den yo' catch yo'se'f a-larfin'
   Till dey hyah yo' 'arf a mile;

65

Den yo' knees begin to quivah,
    An' yo' might be on a jag,
Fo' yo' feel you're drunk all ovah,
    When Lindy plays—a rag!

I have sot an' watched a preachah
    Try to keep his face in trim;
You could see his breast a-heavin'
    Till it swell' up to de brim;
Den yo' ketch his teef a-shinin',
    An' his jaw begins to swag;
He jes' lif's his voice an' hollers,
    When Lindy plays—a rag!

Hit will drive away yo' troubles;
    Hit will mek yo' want to dance;
Ef yo' don' know how to do it,
    Hit will sholy mek yo' prance!
Nevah saw de birds stop singin',
    But I've seen a lively nag
Cut de buckhead in de stable
    When Lindy plays—a rag!

Ef I evah git to glory,
    An' I hyah de angels sing,
An' I hyah de silver trumpets
    Thoo de cou'ts o' heaben ring,
I will nevah hyah no music
    Dat can please me,—an' no brag,—
Bettah dan de kin' dat's ringin'
    When Lindy plays—a rag!

THE POP-CALL

AND,—oh!—I feel so hahnsome!
Bran' new suit and necktie blue,
Sof' felt hat an' bright tan shoe,
Hair slicked down an' a shinin' front,
Feel lak I could do a stunt,
    And,—oh!—I feel so hahnsome!

Gol' head cane an' a big segyar,—
Comes to bein' a spo't, I'm dar!
Rip-jigger-rigger on de Air Line Road!
Got big sugar fo' to pay mah boa'd,
    And,—oh!—I feel so hahnsome!

Ah'm gwine callin' on mah gal,—
Dead game spo't, mah hansome Sal;
One, two, t'ree, fo'!
Right, lef', an away we go!—
    And,—oh!—I feel so hahnsome!

March! Halt, man, here's de gate!
Ah'm gwine in an' set in state!
R'ared 'way back in de rockin' cheer,
Who but me an' Honey-mah-deer,
    And,—oh!—I feel so hahnsome!

Pahlah's lit, but,—dog mah bones!—
Dar sets dat long-leg ol' Jim Jones,
R'arin' back, sah, jes' lak he
Owned de state o' Tennessee!
One, two, t'ree, fo'!
Lef'! lef'! Away we go!—
    And,—oh!—I feel so—lonesome!

FRIENDLY INTEREST

Y'OUGH' to be glad yo' met me, Jim,
   You're lucky lad fo' true!
Fo' sev'al days Ah've had in min'
   Some'n' to say to you.
Now, don't you t'ink Ah'm jealous, Jim,
   Narry time—No, sir!
Ah really t'ink too much o' mahse'f
   To go git jealous o' huh!

You know you're mighty han'some, Jim—
   "Mean it?" 'Deed Ah do!—
An', r'ally, any kind o' girl
   Ain't good ernough fer you!
A flouncy, fluffy, baby girl
   Can' mek a man a wife;
Fo' sparkin' roun' dey're fine, but not
   To tie up to fer life!

A nice hard workin'man lak you,
   Deserves a happy home;
But sugar kisses melt away
   W'en honeymoons are gone.
A home means work as well as love,—
   To scrub an' patch an' stew;
An' while not braggin' on mahse'f,
   Ah know whut Ah c'n do!

"Don't love dat gal?"   Don't say dat, Jim,
    You t'ink mah eyes can' see?
Now, don't you 'spicion a single time,
    Ah want yo' to mar'y me!
No!   Ah'm not anxious!   Go to huh!
    Hang on huh baby breat'—
"Want me?"   Well, buss me, Jim, an' Ah'll
    Be yo's until muh deat'!

CRISSY

I CALLED at Crissy's cabin home—
  A feast of eyes in store;
Her granny placed a chair for me,
  Before the open door.
But Crissy wasn't in the room,
  Nor anywhere in sight;
Perhaps she loiters by the spring,
  And won't be home till night.

There's not a sound of any kind
  To make me think her near,
And granny does not seem to know
  I've come to see my dear;
And tho' she tries to keep my company,
  And says good things and true,
I came to see another girl,
  And nothing else will do.

And just as I am standing up,
  To try my luck once more,
My Juno steps fullfledged from out
  Behind that cabin door.
She saw me when I turned the lane,
  And joyed to see me come;
But first she hies herself away
  To that queer dressing room.

Next time I miss her when I call,
   I'll be absolutely sure
The little minx is dolling up,
   Behind that very door.

YOUTH

I FIND my manhood strong and steady;
Memory strong and ever ready;
Hearing good and life entrancing;
Something learned, and still advancing;
And yet,—I've lost a fervid flavor,
As though the salt had lost its savor;
A sweetness of the days gone by,
Ever haunts my memory.
Youth, O Youth, why hast thou fled me?
Experience, whither hast thou led me?
'Tis oh, for the warmth of long ago!
'Tis, ah! for the chill of this land of snow!
Oh, for youth's poetry and mystery!
Ah, for manhood's day of prose and history!
I would not lose what God has given,
But my soul-sigh for the bliss of heaven
Is, oh, for the time to come in truth,
When age shall drink at the fount of youth!

DAT SUSIE GAL

Went callin' on dat Susie gal
   'Istidy a'ternoon;
An' mebbe, Ah'm gwi' call again,
   But it won't be very soon!

She los' a good pervider,—
   Ah'm no ordinerry man,—
An' Ah went dar jest a-pu'pose
   Fo' to offah huh mah han'!

"How wuz it?"   Well, Ah tell yo';
   'Twarn't no fault o' hern,
But all de same Ah've shook 'uh,
   An',. say, yo' git me?   Durn!

Ah told 'uh Ah wuz comin',
   So she met me at de doo';
Dressed to kill in silk an' satin;
   She wuz lookin' sweet fo' sho!

De mirrah in de hatrack
   Pictu'ed out a stunnin' pa'r!
She'd a pink upon huh bosom,
   An' a rosebud in huh ha'r.

"Won't you walk into de pahlah?"
  Wid dat fetchin', killin' smile!
An' she raised de winder-cu'tains,
  Sparkin' wif me all de while.

"Have a seat here in de rocker!"
  An' Ah looked aroun' to see;
Hit was some'n' on a platform,—
  Altogethah new to me!

Ah was jubous o' dat contraption,
  But Ah nevah once let on,
So down Ah sot, an' r'ared 'way back!
  But de pesky t'ing,—plague on!—

Nevah stopped! Hit rolled right ovah
  Lak a buggy-wheel down hill;
Flung me double-summersetts,
  An' jammed me 'gin de winder-sill!

Dar Ah wuz!—a wreck, bar gracious!
  Evah bone widin me broke!
'Spenders poppin', buttons flyin',
  Tell yo', man, hit warn't no joke!

"Was Ah hu't?" W'y, mah bloomers bu'sted
  Lak Ah run into a mule!
Wors'n all, dat Susie sniggled,
  Till she larfed out lak a fool!

'Twar' not'n' lef' fo' me to do
  But to ax to be excused;
Mah clodin' ruint, mah feelin's hu't,
  Mah lovin' heart abused!

Ah'm sho it warn't no fault o' mine,
  An' mebbe 'twasn't hern;
But all de same Ah've shook 'uh,
  An', say, yo' git me? Durn!

MISS MELERLEE

HELLO dar, Miss Melerlee!
Oh, you're pretty sight to see!
Sof' brown cheek, an' smilin' face,
An' willowy form chuck full o' grace,—
De sweetes' gal Ah evah see,
An' Ah wush dat you would marry me!
  Hello, Miss Melerlee!

Hello dar, Miss Melerlee!
You're de berry gal fo' me!
Pearly teef, an' shinin' hair,
An' silky arm so plump an' bare!
Ah lak yo' walk, Ah lak yo' clothes,
An' de way Ah love you,—goodness knows!
  Hello, Miss Melerlee!

Hello dar, Miss Melerlee!
Dat's not yo' name, but it ought to be!
Ah nevah see yo' face befo',
An' lakly won't again no mo';
But yo' sweet smile will follow me
Cla'r into eternity!
  Farewell, Miss Melerlee!

HAVE I BUT YOU

I CARE not if the roses fade
   In autumn's chilling dew,
If winter weight be overlaid,—
   Have I but you.

The grass may wither, fade, and fall,
   'Twill bloom in spring anew;
But ah, my sweet, I lose my all
   Have I not you!

In summer's sun, in winter's shade,
   Oh, be thou ever true;
Naught matters much with me, sweet maid,
   Have I but you.

THE DOXOLOGY

'Twas Sunday night at Sugar Hill,
    The message fell like hail;
And this with many a groan and shout
    Had made poor sinners quail.

But every lane must have its turn,
    And as the people say,
Not, "Every cat must have her night,"
    But, "Every dog his day."

Mourners called, collection in,—
    The latter rather scant,—
Lifting his hands the parson said:
    "Dismiss us, Deacon Gant!"

But Deacon Gant, forgetting all,
    And, squatting in the shade,
Was swapping horses, and was now
    About to close the trade.

"Brer Gant! Brer Gant!" from mouth to mouth
    The whispered order ran;
The deacon, very much perturbed,
    Arose and thus began:

"Lawd, mek us truly, humbly thankfu'
  W'at we 'bout to 'ceive!"
(If I ain't gone stark natal mad,
  Ah r'ally do believe!)

"Alas! an' did mah Saviour bleed—
  (Ugh! ugh! now, dat ain't it)
"Hark f'om de tombs a doneful soun'—
  (Ah mus' be hav'n' a fit!)

"Praise God f'om whomse all blessin's flow—
  (Naw, mussy! dat ain't it!
Ah'll try once mo', plague take it all!
  Den, hit or miss, Ah'll quit!)

Now Ah lay me down to sleep—
  To mansions in de—(Hell f-f-f-!)
Ah'm feelin' sort o' sick, Brer Paster,
  Jes' say dat t'ing yo' self!"

THE DEVIL

Jestus hu'ts nobody,
   An' r'ally, on de levul,
Hit's time some good man spoke
   A good word fo' de devul.
Yo' hyah some folks complainin'
   De devul's a'ter dem;
But truf compels de mention,
   Dey're trapsein' a'ter *him*.

Dey crowd his halls an' pahlahs,
   Dey th'ong his games an' parks,
Dey encore all his antics
   An' shout at his remarks;
Dey leave de good folks prayin',
   De preachah in his stan';
An' pay to see de devul
   An' his onholy ban'.

Dey love to tease an' flatter him,
   Rej'ice to hyah 'im sung;
But nevah note a Christ'an—
   Excep' to see 'im hung.
But 'e nevah seems to bothah
   De man whose heart is true.
If you don' plague de devul
   He'll nevah bothah you.

Dough doubtless black an' wicked,
  By good repo't 'tis said
He'll be de means o' bringin'
  A good t'ing to a head.
De devul is a tempter,
  But, fo' de crowd, Ah'm sho
Dat, 'stid o' foll'in' *a'ter* dem,
  He's marchin' on befo'.

THE BAPTIZING

MIGHTY glad Ah got a 'ligion,
  'Cause it please mah Mandy so!
Ought to mek de pahson glad—
  Won' hafter preach at me no mo'!

Ah'd a-been converted sooner,
  But Ah don' know how to swim;
An' de pahson's little fellar,—
  Ah'm mos' twice as big as him!

So Ah've come down hyah to practus
  In dis rivah at mah doo';
Den w'en Sunday bring de preachah,
  Ah'll be ready fo' to go.

Moon jes' clam'in' to de tree-tops,
  Mandy singin' on de hill,
Mah wife, she's sho one good 'oman!—
  Guess Ah bettah tek mah pill.

Ah'll jes' wade into it grad'al—
  "While de angry billahs roll—"
Oh! how proper Mandy singin'!—
  Ugh! ugh! folks, dis stuff is col'!

Lemme set mah teef an' go it!—
   Hyah dem waters roun' me curl!
T'ink Ah'm gwine to mek it lovely!
   "Ah'm a-rollin' thoo dis onfriendly worl'!"

Now she clam'in' to mah ahm-pits!
   Gosh! Ah mos' done reach mah size!—
Guess Ah'll sing along wid Mandy,
   He'p to keep mah nerves in ca'm:

"Here's anothah one come to be baptize,
   Be baptize, be baptize,
Here's anothah one come to be baptize,
   Unto the dyin' lam'!"

Guess Ah'll wade a leetle furder!
   Now she lickin' roun' mah chin—
Whoop! Murder! He'p! O Lordy!
   Some'n' done slip, an' Ah'm fell in!

Mandy!—*Pooh h-h!*—Hey dar, you 'oman!
   Come 'ere quick, you hear?—
Suff'rin' saints!—Whoop-p-p!—B'lieve Ah'm
     drownin'!
   Whoop-e-e! Mandy! Come 'ere, dear!

"Now Ah lay me!"—What's gwi' happen?
   Mandee-e!—Uhm-m-m!—You stop dat fuss!
Me hyah drownin'! You dar singin'!
   Ever' minute wuss' an' wuss'!

Heh, you dar, you blame fool nigger!—
   Wush Ah had yo' by yo' ho'n,
Fling you 'alf way cross de rivah!—
   Goo'-by, goo'-by, folks, Ah'm gone!

Umph! Out! Bref—done—lef'—me!
   Swallowed almos' 'alf de stream!
Bet yo' life Ah'm done wid swimmin',
   'Thout Ah do it in a dream!

Yonder come dat Mandy squawkin':
   "Pull, poo' sailor, fer de sho'!"
Wush she drap into de rivah!
   Bet yo' life Ah'd let 'er go!

W'at dat you say 'bout de preachah?—
   Come to see me 'bout mah—what?
Look hyah, gal, jes' say "baptizin',"
   An' Ah'll murder yo' on de spot!

THE SERMON ON THE MOUNT

FOLKS say de Sermon on de Mount
Won't work a-tall, an' 'tain't no count;
But dey won't lak you any day
Onless you do jes' w'at it say!

"Givin' up coats" don' work no mo'!
Tekin' 'em now is all de go!
But dey'll 'fault you on evah side
Onless yo' gi' 'em up yo' hide!

"Goin' 'em two" jes' meks 'em smile!
An' dey won' go you 'alf a mile!
But hyah 'em snortin' evah day
Onless you go dem all de way!

An' "lendin'"? Yo' can' bor' a dollar!
Jes' try it now an' hyah 'em holler!
But w'en dey come, whethah col' or hot,
Yo' mus' han' 'em ovah all yo' got!

An' dis 'ere talk 'bout bein' meek,
An' whiskin' roun' de othah cheek,
Folks say dat hit's a bad on', too,—
But yo' bettah, or dey'll git mad wif you!

86

BUSINESS RELIGION

Yo' c'n *talk* about religion,
　　Good t'ing, too;
But to put it into practus
　　Won' do!

Lookout fo' Number One,
　　Fur ez you c'n see!
Bother with yo' neighbor,—
　　Tha's me!

Nevah lose a minute
　　Wid de thievin' poo';
Bubber, dat ain' business,
　　Tha's sho!

Honesty's a fiction,
　　Policy's de go;
Evahbody's doin' it,
　　Wha's mo'!

Preachahs ain' preachin' it,
　　But dey're livin' it;
We're all hypocrites,
　　Mo' yit!

Fasn' to yo' money!
  Le' me tell yo' twice:
Yo' jes' can' live
  Lak Chris'!

Ketch a fellar nappin',
  Hol' 'im to de light;
Buil' up yo' own se'f,
  Tha's right!

Nevah tetch a fellar
  Tumblin' to 'is fall;
Or you're not'n' *but* a Chris'an,—
  Tha's all!

THE NEW PREACHER

Y'ORTER been to chu'ch dis mornin',
   'At's all Ah got to say:
Tell yo' what, dat colored preachah
   Sho did preach to-day!

Mon, he walked de walls o' Zion,
   Some'n' sweet an' prime,—
"W'at de tex'?" Well, Ah forgit,
   But 'e sho did preach one time!

Ah've hyard lots o' pow'ful sermons,
   Ah mighty well recall;—
"W'at de subjic'?" Don't remember;
   Dis one heads 'em all!

Saint an' sinner got a blessin',
   Ever' word was true;
"W'at 'e say?" Well, 'clar' to gracious,
   Done forgit dat, too!

Ah know he made me shoutin' happy!
   Dat's still widin mah reach!
All de res' done gone an' lef' me,—
   But, honey, he sho did preach!

BAP! TISM!

AH tek mah tex' dis mornin'
    F'om de 'Pistle o' 'Postle John:
He was a Hard-shell Baptis',
    Long 'fo' he was bo'n.
But dat's anothah quest'on;
    Ah'm gwine to prove to-day,
Dat 'e baptize folks
    In de Hard-shell way.

Mah tex' says here,—
    Widout a spark o' doubt,—
Dat 'e went straight in,
    An' 'e come straight out.
If dat ain' what 'e meant,
    It's jes' what 'e said;
An' it sho don' mean
    A little watah on yo' head!

An' Ah notus Pedo-Baptis',
    Clear ovah all de lan',
Don' go into de watah
    Wid a pitcher in dey han'.
But Ah got a proof dis mornin',
    Dat'll enter in yo' eye;
An' if it don't convince you,
    Ah can' see why.

Ain' nobody doubts
   Erbout de soul's conversion;
An' Ah don' see why dey should
   'Bout de body an' ermersion.

Ah git mah testermony
   F'om de Bible on de she'f;
But Ah got a long sight bettah one
   F'om de watah se'f.

An' Ah wan' 'o have yo' notus
   Dat dis 'er ain't no ism;
Fo' yo' back says, "Bap!"
   An' de watah says, "tism!"

FACTS ABOUT LIES

Of all the facts about a lie,
  I've been surprised to know
How quickly they can get around,
  How fast and far they go.

While Truth is doubling up in bed
  To push the cover down,
The Lie is dressed and out and gone,
  And half-way over town.

A lie is easy to believe,
  But Truth is hard to swallow;
A lie will bring a thousand pounds,
  Where Truth can't fetch a dollar.

Truth is like a terrapin;
  A lie is like a bird;
A lie will catch the eye of men,
  Where Truth's nor seen nor heard.

Some people are Missourians,
  But most of them, I fear,
Never believe a thing they see,
  But only what they hear.

A lie can be preposterous,
  The Truth may catch and bell it;
The lie needs do one only thing:
  Just get some one to tell it.

A lie and Truth fell in a wood,
  The world went passing by;
They shouldered Falsehood, took him home,
  And left poor Truth to die.

Truth screamed out in the market place;
  His voice around him whirled;
A liar whispered and his voice
  Was heard around the world.

These are some facts about a lie,
  Enough to show the sin
Of speaking carelessly, and, too,
  Repeating things of men.

SAN JUAN!

Oн, list the stirring story
 That is told of San Juan!
Of Roosevelt's Rough Riders,
 And the fate they fell upon!

This hill, the point of vantage,
 Withstood a bold attack
From tried and trusty soldiers,
 And these had fallen back.

The colonel, through his glasses,
 Had seen it from afar;
He drew nigh with his cavalry
 And loosed his dogs of war.

"Up, men!" the colonel shouted,
 "The block-house on the hill!"
He spurred his charger forward!
 They followed with a will!

Oh, 'twas a gallant company
 Rode up the hill that day!
They never had been daunted,
 Nor ever brought to bay!

But they met a hail of bullets
  No mortal flesh could stand;
And, so, for once retreated,
  A decimated band.

From tree-top, trench, and cactus,
  The leaden shower poured,
While from the smoking block-house
  The deadly cannon roared!

"Halt, company!" See the colonel's face
  All deadly set, and grim!
" 'Bout face!" Once more they're charging
  That fated hill with him!

But galling fire pours fore and aft,
  Which levels horse and men;
They fall as fast as they advance,
  And, so, must down again!

Again the colonel's orders, "Halt!"
  Once more they face about!
Once more they meet that deadly fire
  And still more deadly rout!

But help is nigh! A band strikes up
  Down there upon the right;
And when they come there'll surely be
  "A hot time—in the old town—to-night!"

Who are these sable boys in brown
　　That dare to take the place
Of Roosevelt's Rough Riders,
　　And hope to win the race?

They charge afresh! They charge and sing!
　　They neither shrink nor shirk!
They'd charge the very Gates of Hell,—
　　But singing at their work!

It hailed! It rained! It belched! It blew!
　　That storm of fire and lead!
They sang! They fell! They fairly flew!
　　But always straight ahead!

"To the rear!" their captain shouted,
　　And thitherward went he!
His men went pressing up that hill,
　　As straight as straight could be!

They never wavered! Up, and up
　　They sang and staggered, till
They reached the top, and nobly took
　　That block-house on the hil!

All hail the gallant Twenty-fourth!
　　The band that day played right:
They prophesied it, and there was
　　"A hot time—in the old town—to-night!"

BLACK MAMMIES

If Ah evah git to glory, an' Ah hope to mek it thoo,
Ah expec' to hyah a story, an' Ah hope you'll hyah it,
    too,—
Hit'll kiver Maine to Texas, an' f'om Bosting to
    Miami,—
Ov de highes' shaf' in glory, 'rected to de Negro Mammy.

You will see a lot o' Washington, an' Washington again;
An' good ol' Fathah Lincoln, tow'rin 'bove de rest o'
    men;
But dar'll be a bunch o' women standin' hard up by de
    th'one,
An' dey'll all be black an' homely,—'less de Virgin
    Mary's one.

Dey will be de talk of angels, dey will be de praise o'
    men,
An' de whi' folks would go crazy 'thout their Mammy
    folks again;
If it's r'ally true dat meekness makes yo' heir to all de
    eart',
Den our blessed, good ol' Mammies must 'a' been of
    noble birt'.

If de greates' is de servant, den Ah got to say o' dem,
Dey'll be standin' nex' to Jesus, sub to no one else but
    Him;
If de crown goes to de fait'ful, an' de palm de victors
    wear,
Dey'll be loaded down wid jewels more dan anybody dere.

She'd de hardes' road to trabel evah mortal had to pull;
But she knelt down in huh cabin till huh cup o' joy
    was full;
Dough ol' Satan tried to shake huh f'om huh knees wid
    scowl an' frown,
She jes' "clumb up Jacob's ladder," an' he nevah drug
    huh down.

She'd jes' croon above de babies, she'd jes' sing when
    t'ings went wrong,
An' no matter what de trouble, she would meet it wid
    a song;
She jes' prayed huh way to heaben, findin' comfort in de
    rod;
She jes' "stole away to Jesus," she jes' sung huh way
    to God!

She "kep' lookin' ovah Jurdan," kep' "a-trustin' in de
    word,"
Kep' a-lookin' fo' "de char'et," kep' "a-waitin' fo de
    Lawd,"
If she evah had de quavah of de shadder of a doubt,
It ain't nevah been discovahed, fo' she nevah sung it out;

But she trusted in de shadder, an' she trusted in de shine,
An' she longed fo' one possession: "dat heaben to be
  mine";
An' she prayed huh chil'en freedom, but she won huhse'f
  de bes',—
Peace on eart' amids' huh sorrows, an' up yonder heab-
  enly res'!

BACK TO THE FARM

To Dr. Washington

THE vision of a prophet
   Was yours the day you said:
"Train skillful hands to labor,
   As well as heart and head."
But a wiser word you uttered
   When, stretching forth your arm
And pointing to the cities,
   You said: "Back to the farm!"

Speak louder yet, and louder,
   Till you pierce the cities' noise,
And thunder down the alleys,
   To halt the girls and boys.
Then be a true pied-piper,
   And lead them, not to drown,
But away back in the country,
   And far away from town.

This word must be the trumpet
   To call us from our graves,
Where, buried in the cities,
   We're still a race of slaves.

The Second Call to Freedom,
  Proclaim from state to state;
And let the people answer,—
  Before it is too late.

CHILDHOOD AND YOUTH

THAT FELLOW BEHIND THE GLASS

The fellow that looks at me,
  Behind the looking-glass,
And seems to read my soul
  Right through each time I pass,—
Who is he? What's his name?
Whence comes he? Where, the same?
He seems to know me well;
Better than I could tell;
I'm sure he knows my past,
  As well as what I am.
I dread his piercing eye,—
  He thinks me quite a sham.

I always find him there,
  Whene'er I chance to look,
And, every time, I say:
  "He knows me like a book!"
I think I'd best be good
While in his neighborhood,
Or he will cause me shame,
By singing out my name.
He'd blow my secrets out,
  And publish all my woes,
That fellow behind the glass,—
  For I am sure he knows!

STINGS

"Pull out the sting before it swells,"
    Said dear Mamma to me
One day when I was sorely stung
    From meddling with a bee.
I tweezered out the little hair,
    And down I let it fall;
Then watched to see the swelling come—
    It never came at all!

Since coming into man's estate,
    Her proverb serves me still:
When friends let fly the stinging word
    That would our friendship kill,
I pull the sting before it swells,
    When out a laugh I call;
I've watched to see the swelling come—
    It never comes at all!

THE GIANT

Near our house there dwells a giant
   Nearly fifty cubits high;
Every night we sit and watch him
   As he looms against the sky.

Two great eyes look down upon you,
   From his haystack of a head,—
Eyes that never close in slumber,
   For he never goes to bed.

One long arm he stretches from him,
   One he keeps close to his side;
Slender legs hold up his body
   Many cubits long and wide.

Still he stands in gentle weather;
   In the storm he bows his head;
Never walks for years together,
   'S if his feet were made of lead.

Only after dark he's human,
   With the signatures and signs
Of a weird, stupendous giant:
   In the day, he's two tall pines!

THE POEM IN THE MOON

PAPA, there's a poem in the moon to-night.
Come, look and see how he shines so bright!
Write down, "the close of a sweet June day,"
Write down, "the whippoorwill calling away."

Don't leave out "the calm of the evening hour,"
Nor "the scent of the rose and the jessamine flower";
Put in "the katy-did's one-tone song,"
As they sing all round in a numberless throng;

"The calf's bell tinkling away in the lot,
And the crunching of corn in the selfsame spot;
The flow of the fountain falling afar,"—
You know how it ought to be done, Papa.

Make it all lovely and calm and cool,
And let me sit by you here on a stool,
Gazing up into the moonlit sky
Watching the bats go dipping by.

Leave open doors and windows, too;
Low lights,—yes, and falling dew.
Put Scorpio just above the steeple,
With the bark of dogs and the hum of people;
But over it all pour the moon's soft light,
And leave him there shining thru all the night.

SIGNPOSTS

"SAY, Father, in the path of life
    We tread from day to day,
Are there no signposts on the road
    To keep us to the way?
The bypaths we so often meet,
    Must we them tread, to know
That they are wrong,—then turn our feet
    Back where they ought to go?"

"My son, a guidepost stands in sight,
    The lengthened way along;
If you will read, and read aright,
    You'll find it says: 'It's wrong!'
Where'er this sign comes to your view,
    Though pleasant seem the way,
Know that that path is not the true
    That leads to better day.

"And if sometimes you hesitate
    Because of fading light,
Read in the dust down at your feet,—
    You'll find these words: 'It's right!'
No matter where this path may lead,
    Up to your latest breath,
Seize on it with your utmost speed,—
    It's safe for life,—or death."

A FATHER'S REPLY TO A SON'S QUESTIONS

"My Father, my Father, in getting about,
  Some folk are a trouble to me!"
"This world, my son, is a world of worry,
  But say what yours may be."

"What shall I do when the haughty man
  Looks over or down on you?"
"My boy, that's easy: Why, throw out your chest
  And be a highbrow, too."

"What shall I do when the idle rich
  Flaunt their wealth in your very face?"
"Why, work, and save, and step by step,
  Come to a rich man's pace."

"And the wise old guy who knows it all,
  And singles you out for a fool?"
"My son, his knowledge is always small,
  Meet him by study and school."

"And some you meet are so very good,
  They fill your soul with fear."
"That's the finest task of all the lot:
  Just go him one better, my dear."

"My Father, my Father, give me a rule
  To fill my soul with joy."
"Do only your best, be just to the rest,
  And assert yourself, my boy."

DRINKING SONG

Here we go with a jug of rum!
We're going off on a jolly bum;
    We'll off with the mask,
    And down to the task
Of making the sad world hum.

Here we go with a pack of cards;
We'll leave the parson our best regards:
    In a social way
    We'll spend the day,
Nor give a thought to his canards.

Here we go with a ribald song
To keep the hours from growing long;
    We'll laugh and joke
    In a cloud of smoke,
Nor think for once we're doing wrong.

Here we go till late at night!
We'll be carried home in a sorry plight;
    But till it's done,
    We'll have our fun,
And end the thing with a friendly fight.

Here we go to the prison cell!
The man was killed, but who can tell
    Who struck the blow
    That laid him low?
For no one saw him when he fell.

The sentence given is hard to bear;
I might have done it, for I was there;
    It might have been—
    Too late to mend!
So, here we go!—But where?

ON RECEIPT OF G'S PHOTOGRAPH

A WORLD of longing's in those eyes, my Lad.
They used to stop with me; now, past thy Dad,
They're gazing on the mystery of Life,—
Its joys, its hopes, its sorrows, and its strife;
They're asking: "What of all the things to come?"
But what thou questionest is deaf and dumb;
No answer does the Future give to thee
Seeking solution of her mystery.
But, forward! On! Nor o'er thy shadow grope,—
They who look backward lose the path of hope.
The pressing onward will enlarge thy scope
Of vision, and, at length, some day thy gaze
Shall penetrate Life's veil, resolve the maze,—
And thou shalt walk secure in Wisdom's ways.

THE SENSES

Look straight ahead! That's how your eyes are set;
The danger from behind dare to forget!
Foe, friend, or enemy, worthy of your steel,
Will meet you at the front, not at your heel.
Listen at each side: The future and the past
Will come within your hearing, first and last.
Choose well, and sparingly the things you taste,
Else you admit a foe, your life to waste.
Smell deeply, greedily, the sweet things of the day;
If noxious, 'tis not hard to turn away.
Feel—thoroughly,—your nerves are everywhere.
To feel for all should be your constant care.
You may be blind and deaf and be a man,
But, without sympathy,—I hardly think you can!

ENCOURAGER

To Rev. H. H. Proctor, D.D.

"ALTHOUGH you're not my equal,
   I like to help a man;
And so I tolerate you.
   Go, do the best you can;
You're nothing but a bubble;
   And pretty soon you'll burst.
Folks say bad things about you,—
   And I believe the worst."

That's how some folks impress you,
   Of the way they think of you;
And your schooner takes backwater,
   When their steamers loom in view.
Sometimes you meet another,
   Looks you squarely in the eye,
And says: "My friend, you're special!
   And I see no reason why

"You mayn't tread the Path of Fortune,
   Straight to the House of Fame.
Up! At it! You are extra!
   List up, and win the game!"

And you feel well-nigh invincible,
    When Encourager's about;
God bless the man who heartens,
    And seeks to draw you out!

THINGS DON'T STAY ONE WAY

WHEN darkness hovers o'er the earth,
　　And clouds bedim the day,
I'm ne'er discouraged, for I've learned
　　That things don't stay one way.

When Fortune frowns upon my path,—
　　With hard work, little pay,—
I toil in patience and I wait,
　　For things don't stay one way.

Whene'er the proud go dashing by,
　　In princely-grand array,
No iron pierces through my soul,
　　For things don't stay one way.

The days, the months, the years, all change,
　　Things increase or decay;
Eternal Wisdom has decreed
　　That things don't stay one way.

NELSE

Saw Jim Hedd's niggers goin' souf
   'Istidy, some'n' a'ter break o' day,
Was lookin' in de drivah's mouf,
   W'en 'e give de word to march away!
"W'at 'e sell 'em fo'?" God knows, honey,—
   Hyard 'e had to raise some means;
'Spose 'e jes' mus' git dat money!
   T'irteen,—sol' to New Orleans!

"Was Nelse 'mong 'em?" God, yes! Gone!
   Stronges', hearties' fellar on de place!
You'll miss 'is voice a-singin' in de co'n!
   You'll miss 'is happy, shinin' face!
"How 'e seem to tek it?" Humph!
   Ah wush Ah had de gif' to tell!
But tellin' yo' plain, de bes' Ah mek it,
   Nelse wuz dyin' an' a-gwine to hell!

Partin's allus grievin' day,
   Dough frien's mus' part wid dyin' breat'!
But tearin' bosom frien's away,
   Dat kind o' partin's wors'n deat'!
Nelse givin' up Dinah; Dinah, Nelse,—
   Talk of a mothah an huh chil'!
But man an' wife,—dat's some'n' else!
   Hit made dat boy go jes' plumb wil'!

Mar'ied come Chris'mas jest one year;
　　Cou'tin' since dey mos' could see;
Nevah a couple to each mo' dear
　　Dan Nelse an' Dinah 'pear to me!
Ol' Miss, Ol' Mars', Miss Sallie, an' Miss Fan'
　　Stood on de stoop to see 'em go;
Dinah, huh apron in huh han',
　　Wuz leanin' 'gains' de big-'ouse doo'.

Nelse fixed 'is eyes upon de gal,
　　An' marched off back'ard to de gate;—
No eyes fo' anyt'ing a-tall,
　　But Dinah, 'is sweet'eart an' 'is mate.
He waved 'is han' an' kep' a-wavin',
　　Till 'e struck de big road to de bridge;
Struggled hard, and kep' f'om ravin',
　　Till de road comes to dat willer ridge,

Den Nelse begun to sing: "Farewell,
　　Dinah, mah Honey, mah Darlin', good-by!
God bless you, Honey, mah Love, farewell,
　　Ah'll meet you some day in de sky."
De res' took up de song an' sung
　　Wid swellin' th'oats, till dey reach de ben'
Beyan' de bridge! De music rung
　　As dough de song would have no en'!

"Dinah, mah Honey, mah Darlin', good-by!
　　God bless you, Honey, mah love, farewell!
Ah'll meet you some day in de sky!"—
　　Echoed ovah an' ovah f'om de dell;

Eb'ryt'ing in de chime begun to rebble,—
   De water, meadah, de hill, an' de plain:
De shoals sung bass, de mill-wheel treble,
   De dead leaves whispered in quavahs of pain!

But jest as dey reach de tu'n o' de road
   Dat hides de big-'ouse f'om yo' sight,
De risin' sun bu'st thoo de clouds,
   Bombin' de little ban' wid light!
Wid one acco'd dey stop! Dey tu'n aroun',
   To git de las' look of de ol' home place;
Dey shade deir eyes into a frown,
   De tears a-streamin' down each face!

De women scream, men wep' aloud,
   De drivah kep' proddin' on de crowd;
But Nelse stood still, lak 'e made o' stone;
   An' dem close by 'im hyard 'im groan.
His eye took on a savige light!
   His voice was raised to double might!
His nose, a dancin' adder spread,
   Lak serpent hissin' out 'is head!

Hit rooted me right whar I stood!
   Hit steeled mah ha'r! Hit froze mah blood!
Hit 'peared to shake de solid groun',
   Fo' deat' an' hell was in de soun'!
As 'e lif' 'is han' an' p'inted to de sky,
   De trumpet tones rung out on high,
Dey rose an' fell lak sledge an' hammah:
   "God damn de state of Alabama!"

To mah dyin' day Ah'll nevah forgit it!
'Twas horr'ble! wicked! awful! an' yit it
   Sounded not an o'th,—hit rang out lak a prayer!
Lak t'under out f'om a shinin' sky,
W'en lightnin' hits de tree you're by,
   Hit 'lecterfied us, seemed to 'lecterfy de air!

Dinah drapped down lak somebody dead!
   Ol' Miss run screamin' thoo de doo'!
But whut Ah wuz watchin' wuz ol' Jim Hedd:
   His red face wuz a sight fo' sho!
Ah watch 'im as a tear come in 'is eye,
   An' quickly tu'nin' in 'is track,
Ah hyard 'im say wid a tremblin' sigh:
   "Ah'm gwi' to buy dat nigger back!"

WHATEVER IS IS BEST

SOMETIMES when storms of trouble roll,
    And waves of trial beat
With all their fury o'er my soul,
    They bring me to defeat:
Till comes the calm, as come it will,
    And looking back, I see,
That, spite of either good or ill,
    Whatever is is best for me.

Sometimes my faith grows dead and cold,—
    No hope, no sure retreat,—
And like a sheep without the fold,
    I faint with thirst and heat;
Till spreads the feast, as spread it will,
    And, looking back, I see
His bounty filling all my soul,—
    Whatever is is best for me.

Sometimes deep shadows cross my path,
    Down in the valley low;
Sometimes the billows of His wrath
    Above me overflow;
Till comes relief, as come it will,
    And looking back, I see
His rod and staff my comfort still,
    Whatever is is best for me.

And so I'll trust Him all my days,
　　And take whate'er He sends;
Come life or death, on all His ways
　　My thankful soul depends;
And when He comes, as come He will,
　　I, looking back, shall see
From yon blest height,—forever, still,—
　　Whatever is is best for me.

TIME

TIME is very short.
  Take it by the year,—
Take them by the hundred,
  Shorter they appear.

Time is very long.
  Take it by the day,—
Longest time of all,
  As the seconds tick away.

SEAWARD

To whom shall I leave my boy
  When the ship pulls down the bay,
On the swiftly ebbing tide,
  To land far, far away?

To whom shall my dim eyes look,
  When the boat sinks out of sight?
Who'll foster my eldest born,—
  Out yonder in the night?

There's no one else but God,
  And His sufficiency;
Who guards me on the land,
  Will keep him on the sea.

Here let me safely rest
  My troubled heart and brain:
In Him we separate,
  In Him we meet again.

INSURED

"Insured?" 'Gainst everything!
 "Company?" Moses' rod.
"Place?" The New Jerusalem.
 Yes; I'm insured with God.

He hedges me round with angels;
 Keeps me in all my ways;
Makes my bed in sickness,
 With mercy crowns my days.

I've put my gems and property
 Completely in His hands;
With policies maturable,
 To ev'ry hour's demands.

He's really more than able
 To keep against that day,
Whate'er I put upon Him,
 Along life's toiling way.

From every kind of evil,
 He gives you His protection;—
Sometimes Ten-Dollar funerals,
 But a Billion Resurrection!

GETTING THINGS

WHEN you want a thing you must go and get it,—
  On land or under the sea,—
Whether fortune or fame, or muscle or game,
  No matter what it may be.
If it's down in the ground you must delve for it;
  If up in the air, you must fly;
Some things come to you with length of life,
  To win others you've got to die.

You may not wait for another man
  To share with you his luck,—
Things come to the man who is up and away,—
  The thing that wins is pluck.
  The fellow that comes to bring you a thing,
  Has come to get one, too;
And the fellow that comes to bring you a thing
  Will get the better of you.

You may not wait for your ship to come,
  You've got to fetch her in;
Up! Hoist your sails! Wait not for the breeze!
  Right now is time to begin!
When you want a thing you must go and get it,
  At a time when it may be had;
For Time cannot wait, and the Golden Gate
  May close and leave you sad!

THE IRON RULE

SOME folk stand for pedigree,
   Or else they call for fame,
And if a man is recognized
   Depends upon his name.
But there's not a thing in pedigree,
   There's nothing in a name:
You treat me like a gentleman,—
   I'll treat you just the same.

For you might wear a broadcloth suit,
   And sport a golden cane;
Or you might be the President,
   With power to order rain;
If I passed by in ragged coat,
   Or to your palace came,
If you turned up your nose at me,—
   I'd treat you just the same!

I fancy those who fancy me;
   Good will to friends I show;
But if you do not fancy me,
   Why,—goodness, gracious!—go!
I'd rather be a jelly-fish,
   Alone in all the sea,
Than dwell with you in paradise,
   If you are rude to me.

I'm sure to treat you like a man,
    Whate'er your pedigree;
Yet should you treat me as a fool,
    Then you're a fool to me.
The man I judge a gentleman
    Is he that treats me so;
And he that takes me for a fool,
    Is one himself, I trow.

I do not care for patronage,
    Flatter me,—if you can,—
But all I ask a man to do
    Is: "Treat me like a man."
And if you find you can't do that
    When I'm within your call,
Just pass on by,—I do not care,—
    And do not speak at all!

But if you're ever kind to me,—
    Do me a friendly deed,—
On this one thing you may depend:
    I'll be your friend in need.
If, though, you chance upon me down,
    And give me a foul poke,
Be sure, if e'er the tables turn,
    That I'll repeat the joke.

Nor shall you treat me well alone,
    Then catch me in a crowd,
Make me the butt of ridicule,
    Taunt me with laughter proud;

Though you excel in irony,
  I'd all your wit surpass,
I'd have you crowned the king of fools,
  And branded as an ass!

"The world is but a looking-glass,—
  You smile, and it's returned;
But sneer upon it, and you'll find
  In turn that you are spurned."
So do not stand on pedigree,—
  There's nothing in a name;
But if you'll treat men like a man,
  They'll treat you just the same.

THE VOYAGE

He grasped my hand as he said: "Farewell!"
  For the ship stood in the bay;
And its bell did sound like a funeral knell,
  As it urged my beloved away.

And I heard a wail as the voyagers passed
  From the shore in a silent crowd,
To the huge black ship, in strange contrast,
  To its sail, so like a shroud!

The air grew dark with a dismal hue;
  A calm o'er all things lay;
As the sea into billows the wild winds blew
  That bore that ship away.

My heart shrunk up, it seemed to me,
  As in woe I saw her sail;
But, at length, I heard: "I'll be with thee!"
  Ring out above the gale.

The sea grew calm as she passed from sight,—
  From the port so like a grave;
But my heart was cheered as my faith grew bright
  In the "still small voice" to save.

I know, though she comes this way again,
  She'll bring my friend no more;
But a similar host will she take within,
  To sail for that selfsame shore.

The course she takes is a way unknown,
  From the Port of Parting Breath;
But she bears each soul to heaven or hell,
  And the name of that ship is DEATH!

A PRAYER

FATHER, let Thy lightest whisper
  Reach mine ear, and touch my heart;
Never let Thy gentlest counsel
  Ever from my soul depart.

Let me hear when danger threatens,
  Just before me in the way;
Let me catch each light commission
  Thou appointest to my day.

Let the softest breath of duty
  Catch my willing, list'ning ear;
And the things to be avoided,
  When Thou warnest, let me hear.

Let me never quench the Spirit,
  As He speaks from day to day;
Ever let me heed His pleading,
  Be His message what it may.

So shall I be led in safety,
  O'er the path Thy Son has trod;
So I'll come at last to Glory,
  To my Saviour,—and my God.

HOMEWARD

I'VE come from out the darkness,
  Direct from God's own hand;
Upon this little island,
  My foot first touches land.
I know not whence I came here,
  I know not where I go;
I know I'm on a journey,
  And this is all I know.

This world is not the country
  Where I must take my stand;
I seek another city,
  In some far distant land;
I'm pausing here a moment
  To catch the air and light;
Just let me get my bearings,
  And I'll resume my flight.

BABY SISTER

"TELL brother John to have the organ back,"
   Said Baby Sister, two years old,
And closed her eyes, and took her flight
   Unto a deathless land of asphodels and gold.

The slow-swift years have sped into the past,
   While age has crept into my heart;
The organ long has ceased to play,
   While at her mem'ry still the tear-drops start.

The home-tree old now shelters other heads,
   Where still the broken organ stands;
While Baby Sister and our family,
   Are gathered, all but me, in spirit lands.

Last night I lay a-dream: A message came
   Along some unseen, wireless track:
"Yes, brother John, the organ's gone;
   But soon you'll get your Baby Sister back!"

WAR CAPS

BEHOLD! The warlike hosts of heaven
  Are gathering in the sky!
A moment's calm before the storm,
  And see his arrows fly!
The clash of far-resounding arms
  Reëchoes, peal on peal;
The air grows dark with nameless dread,
  While terrors o'er me steal.

How small and helpless thing is man,
  When heaven's artill'ry soars!
How like the sport of wind he seems,
  When rage above him roars!
The thunder claps about his feet!
  It rolls along the sky!
The lightning taps yon giant tree,—
  Ah, see his splinters fly!

Shall conq'ring warriors from above
  Come down to rule the plain?
Nay! From the clash of godlike arms
  Descends the gentle rain.
E'en so the wrath of monstrous men,
  From war-encumbered days,
Shall minister like falling rain
  To God's eternal praise!

THE SERMON AND THE SONG

I WROTE a splendid discourse,
  And stood before the throng;
I read it through with grace and force,
  Critics found no wrong;
But not an echo did I wake
  Of worship, praise, or duty;
Success was mine, but just to shape
  A thing of passing beauty.

Again, I wrote a pleasing song,
  And forth I stood to sing;
My tones were clear, my notes were strong,
  And had the cultured ring;
But not a heart was stirred to joy,
  Nor eye to shed a tear;
Chagrined, I threw away the toy
  That had no power to cheer.

But later as I strove in prayer,
  A message gripped my soul,—
A song of triumph seized me there,
  I felt myself made whole:
I spake, and moved a mighty throng;
  I sang, they Christward ran.
I found the sermon and the song
  Must live within the man.

SLEEP

I SANK into a sleep profound,
  Unbroken by a dream;
So deep the night had settled down
  The stars cast not a gleam.
Useless the eye and vain the ear,
  So to my couch I crept;
I lay me down without a fear;
  I long and soundly slept.

Sleep bound me with a weighty cord
  That fettered mind and soul.
Should he forever be my lord?
  Would ne'er he set me whole?
He had his mystic way with me,
  I suffered no abuse;
For just as he had bound me he
  As gently, let me loose.

I lay me down all weak and worn;
  I woke with health and grace;
I looked upon a smiling morn,
  The sunbeams in my face.
So Death will bind me in his turn,
  To find no fear in me,—
For he will loose mine eyes at morn
  Upon eternity.

LIFE

LIFE's a single-handed struggle,
    Where no friend may take a part;
Never in the outward conflict,
    Ever in the mind and heart.
Struggle every day and hour,
    From the cradle to the grave;
Struggling, to become a master,
    Yielding, to become a slave.

In a mortal grasp contending,
    Flesh and blood 'gainst mind and soul,
One must,—quailing, fainting, dying,—
    Leave the other in control.
One must conquer in the conflict,
    Bringing 'tother under ban;
Hard it is to drop the monkey,
    Harder still to be a man.

"It is finished!" must be sounded
    From the good or evil side;
He who first shall take the city
    Ever victor shall abide.
See that self with right is sided,
    All its strength and powers to lend;
Though the fight be fearful, doubtful,
    Good will conquer in the end.

IF WE JUST BUT KNEW

If we just but knew Who's with us
   On this raging sea of life,
When the gale blows like a tempest,
   And the wind cuts like a knife,
No doubts nor fears would daunt us,
   Our hearts would still be true,
No demon's self could flaunt us,
   If—we just but knew.

If we just but knew Who's with us,
   When the deluge is at hand,
When high the seething waters
   Pile upon the shifting sand,
Our minds would still be resting
   On Him who seems asleep;
Who but our faith is testing,
   And safe our souls will keep.

If we just but knew Who's with us,
   When the wind and wave are strong,
And when total wreck seems certain,—
   E'en then a joyful song
Our faithful lips would utter,
   And we, with no ado,
Might walk upon the waters,
   If—we just but knew!

I REST ME IN THE LORD

I REST me in the Lord,
  And patiently I wait,
Though sin may bud and flower;
Though great be Satan's power;
Though hosts of sin may hedge me round,
And thunders shake the solid ground,
No qualms, no fears, disturb my breast,
For in my Lord I sweetly rest,
  And patiently I wait.

I rest me in the Lord,
  And patiently I wait,
While He prepares the way
To usher in the day
When all His children, bright and fair,
Shall rise to meet Him in the air.
So, till He takes me to His breast,
Forever there in peace to rest,
  I patiently will wait.

FIFTIETH ANNIVERSARY

First Congregational Church, Atlanta

Fifty years of service! What a record thine!
Thou hast stood for character, plus the life divine!
Thou'st kept the Great Commission: Opened blinded
    eyes;
Raised the dead and dying; hast garnered in the skies!

But whiter grows the harvest as brighter grows the day;
The call, "Come o'er and help us!" is sounding hereaway;
While from the old Golgotha there still resounds the cry:
He who serves must suffer! He who saves must die!

Yea, hotter grows the conflict as fiercer glows the sun;
Tho' flesh and blood are tottering, the race is just begun;
No rest is to the weary, but only death or dearth
Till Love men's hearts shall conquer, and Justice rule the
    earth.

O First Church of Atlanta! First on Southern soil!
Gird thee still for battle! Trim thee to thy toil!
Pilgrim, bravely onward! Soldier, shirk no pain!
Sympathy comes through suffering! Loss alone is gain!

AT TWILIGHT

I sit at twilight all alone,
   Watching the embers' ruddy glow;
The flame gives out a merry tone,
   Dancing merrily to and fro.
Shadows pall the corners dark,
   Or, fanlike, spread across the room;
And from the deep recesses,—hark!—
   Voices echo from the gloom.

'Tis my mother's voice that speaks,
   Calling my old familiar name;
She comes and strokes my hair and cheeks,—
   I'm child to-night because—she came.
A sister comes, and then another
   Takes her old familiar place;
Two sweet babes and then a brother
   Flit before my yearning face.

Then a sweetheart,—wife, and fellow,—
   Comes my saddened heart to cheer;
Fills my mind with mem'ries mellow,—
   I sweep away the falling tear.
Now they come in troops around me,—
   Friends I followed to the tomb,
Through the twilight come and find me,
   Till they fairly fill the room.

"Shadows," say you?   No, a throng
   Of friends from out beyond the stars;
Who at twilight drop among
   Their friends on earth through golden bars.
Gone the glow of hearth and embers,
   Save the crack of dying coals;
Closed my heart its secret chambers,
   And its treasure of dear souls.

RELIGIOUS BUSINESS

THE wholly true to Christ
  Are ever on the Cross;
He who follows Jesus,
  Daily, suffers loss.

He never can be rich,
  As long as there are poor;
Nor enter world success,
  Because Pride keeps the door.

He may not seek for gain,
  Which is its own reward,—
His treasure is in heaven,
  His boast is in the Lord.

He has a Christly boldness
  To be uniformly good;
So, he rarely pleases men,
  Is seldom understood.

But the Sons of God shall triumph,
  With mighty victory!
For righteousness shall fill the earth
  As waters fill the sea!

Oh, his reaping time is coming,
  With a fullness for his dearth,
When Christ shall have dominion,
  And the meek possess the earth!

Lord, make me pure in heart,
  And resolutely true;
To bear my cross in patience,
  And be numbered with the few.

Help me to plumb the line,
  And "follow" for the nonce;
And never to attempt again
  To walk two ways at once.

THE END